SUPERBASE 2

MIRAMAR

First published in summer 1988 by Osprey
Publishing Limited
59 Grosvenor Street, London W1X 9DA
Reprinted spring 1989 and autumn 1989

British Library Cataloguing in Publication
Data
Hall, George
    Miramar.—(Superbase; 2).
    1. United States. Air bases
    I. Title   II. Series
    358'.4'17'0973
ISBN 0–85045–845–5

Editor Dennis Baldry
Designed by David Tarbutt
Printed in Hong Kong

Front cover LCDR George Korson
prepares to preflight his VF-302
F-14 Tomcat at the start of the day's
flying

Title pages Pacific coast fog slips
toward NAS Miramar at sunset

Right T-2 Buckeye, used for
recurrent stall-spin training of F-14
aircrews

Hot Hornets

Left CDR Jon 'Pops' Green, youthful skipper of VFA-303, the Navy's first reserve squadron to check out in the F/A-18 Hornet (background)

Above A Hornet of VFA-303 taxies for takeoff at Miramar. The extra underwing tanks double the aircraft's range

Top Gun student birds park alongside Hangar One
during their five-week course of instruction

Preceding pages A two-ship of Navy Hornets heads for the Yuma, Arizona, ACM (air combat manoeuvring) range, about 125 km from Miramar

This page The versatile Hornet doubles as a strike bomber as well as a superb fighter aircraft. This Navy Reserve bird sports empty multiple-ejector bomb racks as it returns from a desert bombing range

Above A Hornet plugs into the KC-10's trailing fuel basket. Tanker 'track' is over the Pacific Ocean west of Miramar

Left Brand-new Hornet of VFA-15 'Valions' is assigned to the air wing of the equally new nuclear carrier USS *Theodore Roosevelt*

Reserve Hornets pose beneath the refuelling window of an Air Force KC-10 tanker

Left F/A-18 of VFA-15 'Valions' lifts
easily in military power from the
Miramar runway

This page Dogfighting Hornet puffs
transonic vapour as it pulls heavy
positive G in an ACM engagement

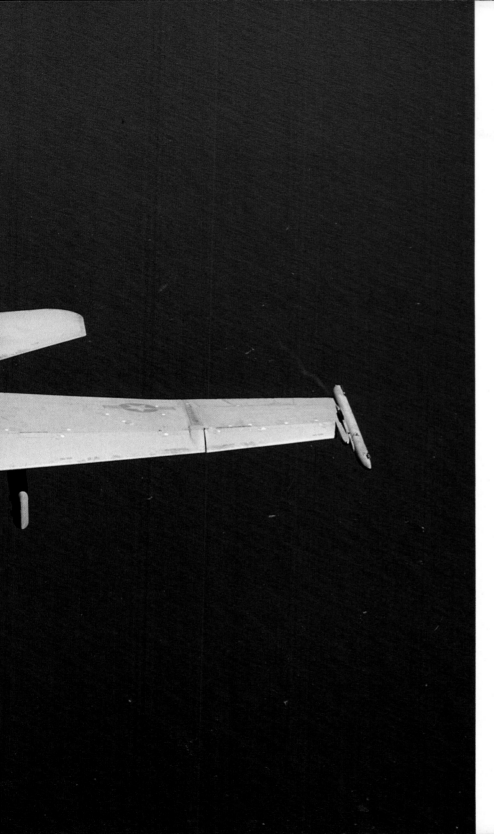

Marine Corps' Hornet of VMFA-323 'Death Rattlers' poses below the open cargo ramp of its companion Marine KC-130 Hercules tanker over the Pacific tanker track

A Hornet driver snaps his wingman
as they head back to Miramar after
an overwater intercept mission

Preceding pages and these pages
Marine Corps' Hornets of VMFA-531 'Grey Ghosts', based at MCAS El Toro, up the freeway from Miramar. Pilot, (right) photographed during his recent stint as a Top Gun student, is Capt John 'Lips' Durkin

This page and overleaf The Navy's crack flight demonstration team, the Blue Angels, transitioned in 1987 to the F/A-18 Hornet after a decade of performing in the little A-4 Skyhawk. These shots were taken at Miramar's annual summer open house and air show

A Marine Hornet runs through ground checks at Miramar prior to a night intercept hop

Marine Capt Tim 'Tiny' Timm (tiny, of course, at 6 ft 4 in) checks his dummy
Sidewinder before a dawn launch

Adversary Falcons

Navy adversary squadrons and Top Gun instructors
are now flying the F-16N Falcon, permitting them to
simulate the hottest bad guys around

Top Gun Falcons are perhaps the world's hottest variants of this great fighter; fitted with the gutsy GE F110 engine (note the different con/di nozzle), they have been stripped of any excess weight—weapons delivery systems, gun, etc

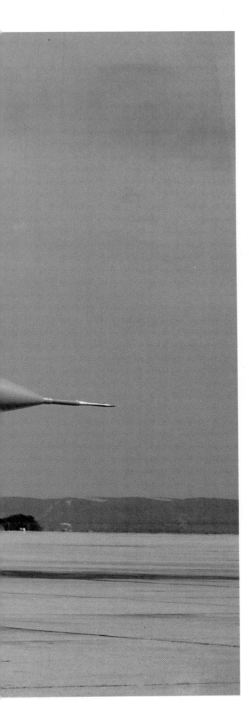

Above Civilian-contract mechanics service the Falcons of the Top Gun school and of the VF-126 'Bandits', Miramar's resident aggressor squadron

Left and overleaf Top Gun dogfighting maestro Ted 'Pyro' Hendricks fires up and heads for the Yuma range, there to make mincemeat of a hapless student

This page Adversary F-16 is joined by a huge F-14 Tomcat for the customary landing 'break' over the Miramar runway. The Falcon is not all that small; it's the Tomcat that's enormous

Aggressor F-5s

Highly-regarded F-5E Tigers are now being retired at Miramar as the new F-16Ns arrive. These Top Gun birds, done up in various Middle Eastern and Warsaw Pact camouflage schemes, will relocate to the fast-growing Naval Air Station at Fallon, Nevada

Main Picture Two-seat Top Gun F-5F waits with a Navy A-4 Skyhawk as a Beech C-12 executive transport dawdles in on an instrument approach

Inset Civilian Northrop mechanic gives the 'light up' sign to Top Gun executive officer LCDR Tom 'Otter' Otterbein in his F-5E

Mongoose

Left Top Gun A-4 gets waved off for another go-around when a large transport is slow in clearing the active runway

Right LCDR Roger 'Muff' Dadiamoff, adversary A-4 pilot with Miramar's Reserve Gomer squadron, VC-13

Below A Navy jet pilot's first carrier landings will be made in a T-2 Buckeye trainer (foreground). The student will then transition to the much hotter A-4 Skyhawk (background) for the remainder of his advanced jet training

The VF-126 'Bandits' operate ancient one- and two-seat A-4 Skyhawks as well as factory-fresh F-16N Falcons

Right A Top Gun A-4 Mongoose, fitted with a huge Pratt & Whitney P-8 engine, lights the wick for takeoff

Below Although designed as a low-level attack plane, the A-4 is a fearsome dogfighter in expert hands. The Top Gun jets have been stripped of all extra weight and stuffed with large P-8 engines, allowing them to stay in the fight with just about anyone

Far right During the filming of *Top Gun* over the California desert, 'Iceman's' F-14 is trailed by Top Gun skipper 'Viper' in an A-4 Mongoose

Top Gun and VF-126 Skyhawks
await their mounts as an E-2
Hawkeye shoots approaches

Left VF-126 Bandit birds carry red stars and large nose numbers in the Soviet mode

Below and right Top Gun and VF-126 A-4s are among the oldest jets in the entire Navy inventory. They are beautifully maintained despite their age, but they require huge amounts of maintenance to keep them operational in the harsh ACM environment

These pages The A-4 Mongoose is painted in a variety of colour schemes which are designed to simulate the warpaint worn by likely threat aircraft around the world

Tomcat

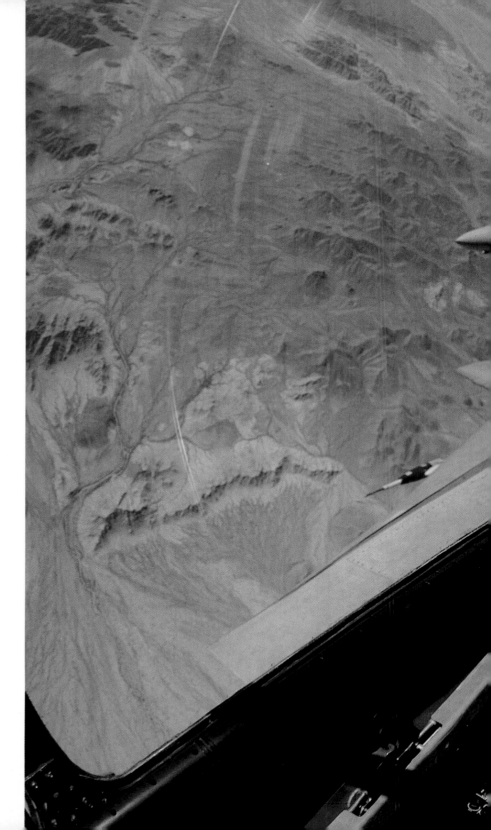

Following pages Tomcats of Miramar's VF-111 'Sundowners' over the lush Imperial Valley of southern California.

This page Tomcat of the Miramar Replacement Air Group, or RAG, the unit which trains brand-new jet pilots in the intricacies of the F-14

Right and overleaf F-14A Tomcat of Miramar squadron VF-124 'Gunfighters' wows the crowd at the Miramar open house. Note different positions of the Tomcat's variable-geometry wings

Main picture Tomcat of VF-194 'Red Lightnings' blasts out of Miramar in full afterburner. This venerable squadron is being dissolved into other Miramar outfits in a cost-cutting move. **Inset** A Tomcat of VF-124 lets it all hang out

Below A RAG Tomcat done up in imaginary squadron markings for the movie *Top Gun*. Maverick's nemisis Lt Tom 'Iceman' Kazansky is at the stick

Left RAG Tomcat turns and burns during the filming of *Top Gun*

Preceding pages and main picture Tomcat of one of Miramar's two Naval Reserve squadrons, the VF-302 'Stallions', poses for the photographer over the Yuma ACM range

These pages, overleaf and following pages F-14 Tomcat of VF-302 photographed below the boom operator's window of a KC-10 Extender tanker

Top photos Tomcat of the VF-124 RAG painted up especially for the 1987 air show tour. Miramar is known throughout American naval aviation as 'Fightertown USA'

Left RAG Tomcat practices touch-and-go landings in the background as an east-coast F-14 awaits its Top Gun student crew

Opposite below and left Impeccable F-14 of east coast squadron VF-84 'Jolly Rogers' parked on the Top Gun student ramp. Zero-zero, or 'double nuts', designation, on tail, indicates that this is the aircraft of the carrier's chief pilot, the Commander of the Air Group, or CAG

Inset Top Gun classes are like a navy fighter pilot convention. Bird on left is from VF-41 'Black Aces', the outfit that bagged two Libyan *Fitters* in the Gulf of Sidra. The others, left to right: VF-102 'Diamondbacks', VF-33 'Starfighters', VF-84 'Jolly Rogers'

Main picture Typical student ramp during a Top Gun class will see visiting birds from as many as ten different F-14, F/A-18, and (for a short while longer) F-4 squadrons

Inset Navy seamen, swabbing down a VF-41 Tomcat, are dwarfed by the immense fighter

Above CAG Tomcat off the carrier USS *America* is readied for a wash

Main picture Miramar Tomcat gets the clean-up treatment as a visiting Marine Corps' TA-4J Skyhawk waits its turn

A Tomcat of one of the long-time
resident Miramar squadrons, the
VF-211 'Checkmates'

Above Plane captain rides the brakes as his F-14, freshly washed, is towed back to the Top Gun student line

Left Two Skyhawk pilots of the VF-126 'Bandits' walk in after a bout of dogfighting. Note mock Soviet insignia on their blue flight suits

On any given day, over a hundred
F-14s will share the mile-long ramp
at Miramar

Below East coast F-14 Tomcat
arrives at the start of a five-week
Top Gun class

Above Reserve Tomcat of VF-302
'Stallions' off the California coast.
Orange pod is a data transmitter
which sends real-time information to
TACTS (Tactical Air Combat
Training System) computers and
displays on the ground. An entire
dogfight can be viewed on this
amazing system

Left Call-signed coffee cups in the
ready room of the VF-302 'Stallions'

This page Detailed briefings lasting over an hour precede virtually every tactical flight out of Miramar. VF-302 skipper CDR John Ed 'Tiger' Kerr, right, is in charge

Right All flying Navy personnel are required to undergo two days of gruelling water survival training every three years. This helicopter crewman is doing his requisite 15 minutes of 'drown-proofing', or treading water, in full flight gear. Try it sometime!

Reservist LCDR George Korson runs
two manufacturing businesses in San
Deigo as well as flying several times
a week with VF-302 'Stallions'

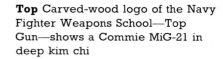

Top Carved-wood logo of the Navy Fighter Weapons School—Top Gun—shows a Commie MiG-21 in deep kim chi

Middle Seated in 'Hollywood' Dishart's Top Gun F-5E is Air Force Capt Joe Leister, guest instructor on the Top Gun faculty

Bottom VF-302 skipper 'Tiger' Kerr about to taxi out

Far left A trio of AIM-7 Sparrow radar-guided air-to-air missiles being loaded onto a Miramar F-14 for a live shoot over the Pacific missile range

A two-ship of VF-302 Tomcats slides easily away from Miramar. The back-seater is squadron flight surgeon Connie 'Doc' Ward, a Vietnam vet in the rear cockpit of the F-4 Phantom

Inset Tomcat pulls the gear as it lights out of Miramar in full afterburner

Main picture Zone V afterburner again, as a VF-154 Tomcat is catapulted from the deck of the carrier USS *Constellation*. Miramar is home base for more than a dozen carrier squadrons—F-14 Tomcats and E-2 Hawkeyes

Right Tomcats motor their huge wings forward as they pull out of the landing break over the Miramar runway

Below Control positions in the TACTS trailer at Miramar. Dogfights over the Yuma range can be observed in real time or taped for later debriefing on the colour displays

Below Close-up of the TACTS display. Birds 1 and 2 are about to call missile shots on the desperately-turning No 3. But they'd better pay attention to No 4, sneaking in low over the Chocolate Mountains!

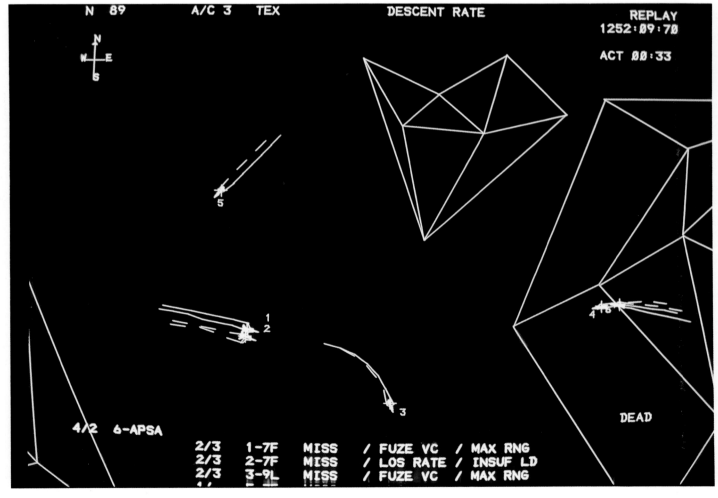

N 89   A/C 3   TEX   DESCENT RATE   REPLAY
                                                     1252:09:70

                                                     ACT 00:33

5

1
2

3

DEAD

4/2 6-APSA

2/3   1-7F   MISS   / FUZE VC   / MAX RNG
2/3   2-7F   MISS   / LOS RATE / INSUF LD
2/3   3-9L   MISS   / FUZE VC   / MAX RNG

Mid-range Sparrow air-to-air missile is fired at a pilotless drone over the Pacific Ocean west of Miramar. Shooter is a Tomcat of VF-302 'Stallions'.

Main picture Miramar's other
tenants, aside from the fighters, are
the Grumman E-2C Hawkeye
airborne early-warning craft. The
bird lifting off is attached to VAW-
114 'Hormel Hawgs'

This picture Miramar Tomcats snap
into a perfect 4G break over the
carrier USS *Constellation*

Tomcat slips in over the strobes as dusk settles on Miramar

On the boat

On the boat Model builders love the VF-21
'Freelancers', a Tomcat squadron that hangs on by the
fingernails to the old-fashioned shiny enamel paint.
This beautiful specimen is circling its home away from
home, the USS *Constellation*

Top left Catapult officer on *Connie* gives the classic 'launch' signal to an F-14. The 30-ton bird will accelerate past 150 mph in just over 2 seconds!

Bottom left 'Freelancers' Tomcat takes a dusk cat shot aboard *Connie*

Main picture Hornets line the foredeck of the USS *Ranger* as a Tomcat is hurled from one of the waist catapults

Blast deflector is raised behind each jet prior to the cat shot. It's no optical illusion: the forward edge of the deck is only 300 feet in front of the pilot!

Left Reserve Hornets, and a lone A-7 Corsair, receive taxi hand signals aboard USS *Ranger*

Above Hornet driver about to get the ride of his life aboard *Ranger*

Below Hornet storms down the port bow cat of *Ranger*; his wingman in the starboard track will be only seconds behind

Preceding pages Now it's the Hawkeye's turn. Nicknamed the 'Hummer', the big turboprop has a reputation for being a terrible handful around the carrier deck

Right The Hawkeye is flown by a crew of two, while three combat controllers man the scopes in back. Fleet-defence fighters are vectored toward potential threats by this trio of 'scope dopes' aboard the Hummer

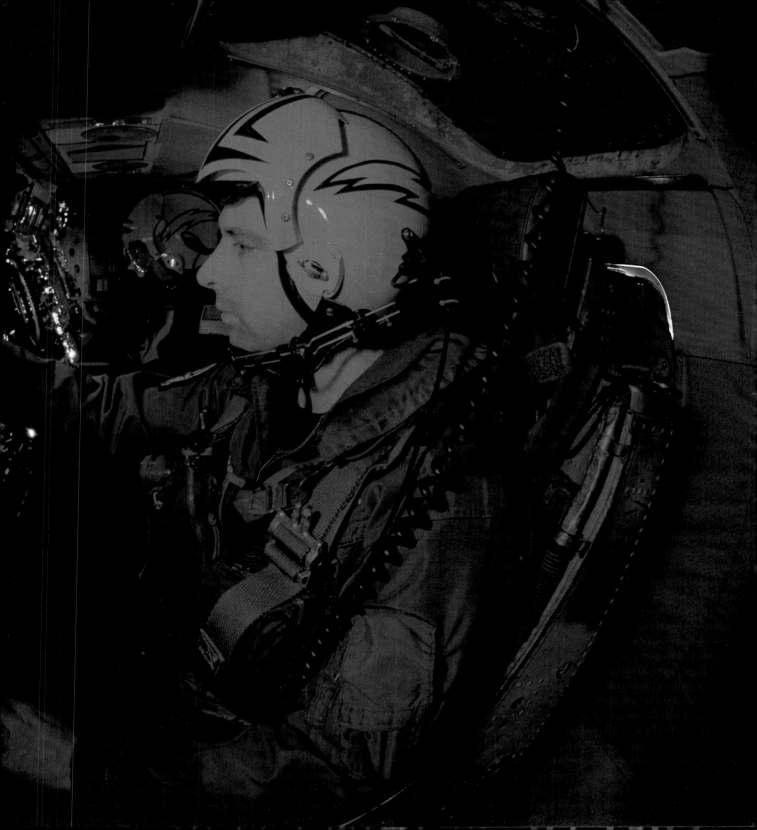

Above A gaggle of radar and radio antennas are contained inside the Hawkeye's rotating dome. The amazing airborne control centre can track anything that moves, on or above the sea, in some 3 million cubic miles of airspace

Right 'Hormel Hawgs' E-2C approaches the boat. All Navy pilots have high regard for Hummer drivers, since the plane is infamous for three-axis squirreliness in the landing configuration

Last page Marine Corps' Reserve F-4 Phantom blasts out of Miramar into a matchless Pacific sunset